HYBRIDS

Cockatiel + Galla = Gallatiel

Naira R. Matevosyan

Copyright © 2014, L'Auteur Librairie

ISBN: 978-1500701000 – CreateSpace, Inc; Seattle, WA

CONTENTS:

Hybrid is the interbred offspring of living species, races, or genera. In the Oxford definition system, the word *hybrid* is derived from Latin *hyba*, as in "*kakapo,* the offspring of an owl and parrot" for example, or if in human species, the "child of a freeman and slave."[1] Hybrids are commonly produced for a desirable phenotype absent or inconsistently present in the parent populations.

The flow of genetic material between populations or races is called *hybridization.* We have to appreciate the difference between the four types of hybridization: (1) genomic, (2) numerical, (3) structural, and (4) permanent.

(1) A *genomic hybrid* carries two different alleles of the same gene. Examples are *cama* - a cross between the camel and lama, *hercules* = lion + tiger,

zonkey = zebra + donkey, *mule* = canary + goldfinch, *zorse* = zebra + horse,

ZORSE

LOWLAND PUGRILLA

Lowland Pugrilla = bulldog + gorilla, *puguin* = bulldog + penguin, or *stockvault wolf* = fox + grey wolf.

PUGUIN

STOCKVAULT WOLF

In genomic or DNA-hybridization, two complementary single-stranded DNA or RNA molecules are combined to form a single double-stranded molecule through base pairing. In fact, this type of hybridization it is an assortative mating or mutation.[2] The prominent scientists, Charles Sibley and Jon Ahlquist, pioneered the use of DNA kinetics to investigate evolutionary relationships using the DNA-DNA hybridization.

Each DNA molecule is made of two strands of nucleotides. If the strands are heated, they will separate — and as they are cooled, the attraction of nucleotides will make them bond back together. The weak bonds can be broken with just a little heat, while closer matches require more heat to separate the strands again.

To compare different species, the DNA of various species are cut into small segments, the strands are separated, and then mixed. When the DNA of two species bond together, the match between the strands will not be perfect since there are genetic differences. The more imperfect the match, the weaker the bond between the two strands. The more closely the two species are related, the fewer mispairings will occur.

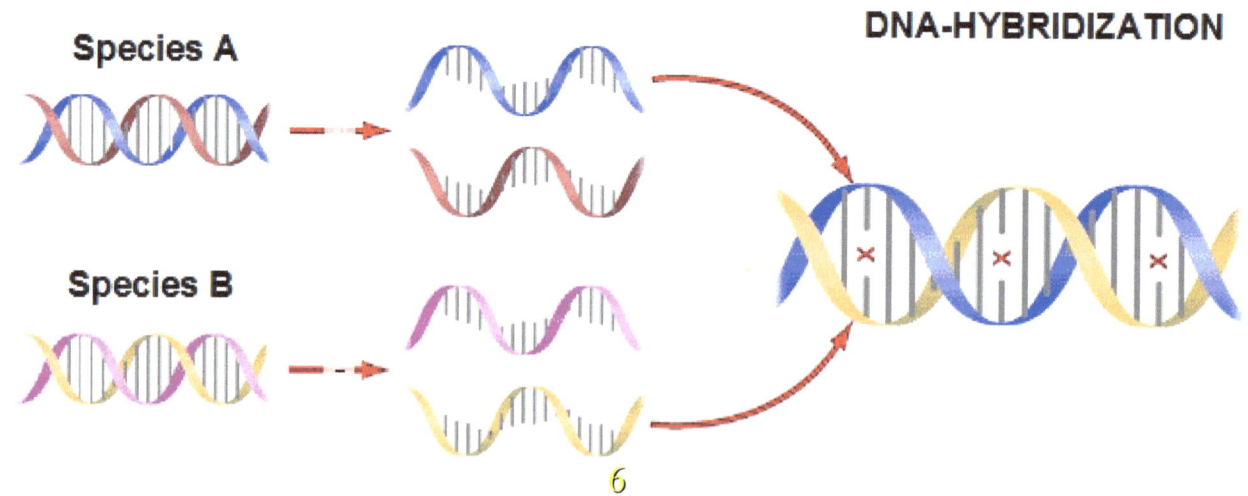

MOLE SALAMANDER

GUINEA FLAWORM

LEECH

BRINE SHRIMP

(2) A *numerical hybrid* is the result of a gametal fusion with different haploid numbers of chromosomes. In fact, we are talking about the *polyploidy*. *Numerical hybridization* can be induced in plants and cell cultures by some chemicals, *colchicine* or *oryzalin*, that double the chromosomes. Naturally,

polyploidy occurs in some animals, like *goldfish, salmon,* or *salamanders,* but is especially common among *ferns* and *flowering plants.*[3]

Polyploidization is a mechanism of *sympatric speciation* because polyploids are usually unable to interbreed with their diploid ancestors. Examples in animals are mostly common in non-vertebrates: *mole salamander, flatworm, leech,* and *brine shrimp.* Some fish have as many as 400 chromosomes.

XENOPUS, THE FROG

Polyploidy was first induced in fish in 1956, by an Indian scientist Har Swarum. He used a cold-shock treatment of the eggs close to the time of fertilization, which produced triploid embryos that successfully matured.[4] Cold or heat shock has also been shown to result in unreduced amphibian gametes. In 1958, John Gurdon, from Hamshire/England, transplanted intact nuclei from somatic cells to produce diploid eggs in the frog

Xenopus, that were able then develop to the tadpole stage.[5]

John Burdon Haldane, the British scientist from Oxford, hailed the work for its potential medical applications, and became one of the first to use the word *clone* in the fauna. Later work by Japanese researcher Shinya Yamanaka showed how mature cells can be reprogrammed to become pluripotent, extending the possibilities to non-stem cells. Gurdon and Yamanaka were jointly awarded the Nobel Prize in 2012 for this work. [6]

According to the number of the chromosome sets in the nucleus, polyploid types are labeled like these:

triploid (three sets; 3*x*), for example seedless watermelons;

tetraploid (four sets; 4x), for example Salmonidae fish;

pentaploid (five sets; 5x), for example Kenai Birch;

hexaploid (six sets; 6x), for example kiwifruit;

heptaploid (seven sets; 7x), for example Elymus Farctus;

octaploid (eight sets; 8x), for example dahlias;

decaploid (ten sets; 10x), for example strawberries;

dodecaploid (twelve sets; 12x), for example Xenopus ruwenzoriensis:

Triploid

Tetraploid

Pentaploid

Octaploid

Hexaploid

Heptaploid

Decaploid

Dodecaploid

While mammalian hepatocytes are polyploid, rare instances of polyploid mammals are known, and most often result in prenatal death. True polyploidy scarcely occurs in humans, although polyploid cells occur in highly differentiated liver parenchyma, heart muscle, or bone marrow. Aneuploidy is more common.[7]

Polyploidy occurs in humans in the form of *triploidy*, with 69 chromosomes (69,XXX), and tetraploidy with 92 chromosomes (92,XXXX). *Triploidy*, usually due to *polyspermy*, occurs in about 2-3% of all human pregnancies and ~15% of miscarriages. The vast majority of triploid conceptions are miscarried; those that do survive to term typically die shortly after birth.

Complete *tetraploidy* is more rarely diagnosed than *triploidy*, but is observed in 1-2% of early miscarriages. However, some tetraploid cells are commonly found in chromosome analysis at prenatal diagnosis and these are generally considered 'harmless'. There are, at any rate, very few clinical reports of fetuses/infants diagnosed with tetraploidy mosaicism.

(3) *A structural hybrid* results from the fusion of gametes that have differing structure in at least one chromosome, as a result of structural abnormalities. It possesses a heterozygous genotype, because all homozygous combinations are lethal. In this type of fusion, gametes have different haploid numbers of chromosomes. It is often seen in divergent and isolated species.

Intrinsic isolation may result from Dobzhansky–Muller incompatibilities, in which deleterious interactions among genes or gene products lead to developmental problems or under-dominant chromosome structure differences between the parents.[8]

Divergent populations become intrinsically and reproductively isolated when hybrids between either these fail to develop properly or do not produce viable offspring. Intrinsic barriers may result from either deleterious interactions among heterospecific genes or gene products or chromosome structure differences that are deleterious in heterozygotes. The moss *Ceratodon purpureus* is an example of structural hybrid:

Moss, CERATODON PURPUREUS

In humans, Chromosome-18 abnormalities, clinically manifested to the Edwards syndrome, may also be seen as linked to this type of hybridization.[9] Edwards syndrome (*Trisomy 18*) named after John Hilton Edwards, who first described the syndrome in 1960, is the second-most common *autosomal trisomy* after Down syndrome, that carries to term. With an occurrence of one out of 6,000 live births, around 80% of the affected are females. The incidence increases as the mother's age increases. Clinics may include kidney malformations, structural heart defects (ventricular septal defect, atrial septal defect, patent ductus arteriosus), omphalocele, esophageal atresia, microcephaly (small cranium), micrognathia (small jaw), ocular hypertelorism (widely spaced eyes), cleft lip/cleft palate, narrow eyelid folds, ptosis (hanging upper eyelids), a short breast bone, clenched hands, choroid plexus cysts, intellectual disability, developmental delays, growth deficiency, breathing difficulties, arthrogryposis (a muscle disorder that causes multiple joint contractures at birth). [10-12]

(4) A *permanent hybrid* is based on heterozygous hybridization, a status quo where all homozygous combinations are lethal. This state is often described as *overdominance* or *heterozygote advantage*.

In general terms, *over-dominance* is a condition where the phenotype of the hetero-zygote lies outside of the phenotypical range of both homozygote parents, and heterozygous offspring has a higher fitness than the homozygous one.

An examples is *Drosophila melanogaster*, hybrid model of a fly known as the common *fruit fly* or *vinegar fly*. This hybrid insect

Drosophila melanogaster

was selected and is widely used in biomedical research and microbial pathogenesis, because it is easy to maintain, has four pairs of chromosomes, breeds quickly, and lays many eggs.

Other vivid examples include *Koolakamba*, *Beefalo*, and *Humanzee*.

The *Koolakamba* or *Kooloo-Kamba* is purported to be a hybrid species of two different apes: chimpanzees and gorillas. This alleged hybrid has been reported in Africa as early as the mid 19th century though to date no scientific evidence has been found to substantiate the existence of the creature and it has no entry in

14

Koolakamba

the NCBI taxonomical database. The *Koolakamba* is believed to be larger, flatter faced, larger skulled and more bipedal than a chimp; though, it may also be a mutation.

Beefalo is a fertile hybrid of domestic cattle, generally a male Bos taurus and female American bison. The breed is created to combine the features of both animals for a better beef production. Crossing a male bison with a domestic cow produces few offspring, but that crossing a domestic bull with a bison cow apparently solves the problem. [13]

Beefalo

Humans have one fewer pair of chromosomes than other apes, with ape chromosomes 2 and 4 fusing into a large chromosome (which contains remnants of the *centromere* and *telomeres* of the ancestral 2 and 4). Having different numbers of chromosomes is not an absolute barrier to hybridization; similar mismatches are relatively common in existing species. Chimpanzees and humans

15

are closely related (sharing 95% of their DNA sequence and 99% of coding DNA sequences), leading to contested speculation that a hybrid is possible. As such, the *humanzee* (also known as the *Chuman* or *Manpanzee*) is a hypothetical chimpanzee - human hybrid.[14]

A *para-human* is a human-animal hybrid or *chimera*. Scientists have done extensive research into the mixing of genes or cells from different species, e.g. adding human genes to bacteria and farm animals to mass-produce insulin and spider silk proteins, and introducing human cells into mouse embryos.

Humanzee

Ilya Ivanov was the first scholar to attempt creating a human–ape hybrid. In 1910, he gave a presentation to the World Congress of Zoologists in Graz, Austria, in which he described the possibility of creating such a hybrid by artificial insemination. Later he was exiled from the Soviet Russia for his other open and bold speeches.[16] Some scholars find that human-animal chimeras or hybrids are threats to the human dignity.[15]

Nevertheless, there are several reasons for which *parahumans* are sought: for medical and industrial purposes, production of drugs and of organs suitable for organ transplantation; for better knowledge of the human physiology, especially the immune and neural system functions. Also, restrictions on cloning and stem cell research have made chimera research an attractive alternative.

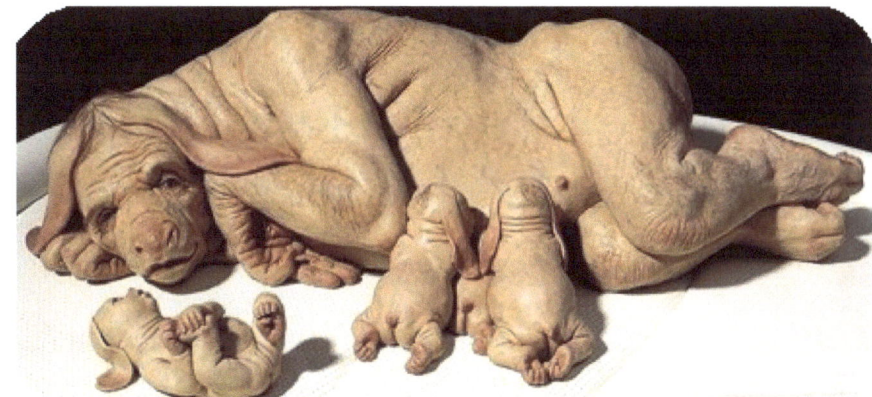

HYPOTHETICAL HUMAN HYBRID

If a line of *parahumans* could be created using germline engineering, they would qualify as a species. *Parahumans* created by somatic genetic engineering would have human children. Another key difference is that a *germ-line parahuman* would have to be modified before birth, while a *somatic parahuman* could be an adult human who chooses to be modified. Which model is more legal or ethical, is a matter of the everlasting debate. An argument for the former is that *no harm is done to a person born with modified genes because the person would have had no control over their genes in the first place.* An argument for the latter, being more ethical, is that *the changes would be made with informed consent.*

In the United States, H.R. 5910 is a House Resolution entitled *Human-Animal Hybrid Prohibition Act* of 2008.

All great apes have similar genetic structure in terms of the chromosomes 6, 13, 19, 21, 22, and X. Chromosomes 3, 11, 14, 15, 18, and 20 match between gorillas, chimpanzees, and humans. Chimpanzees and humans match on 1, 2p, 2q, 5, 7-10, 12, 16, and Y. This degree of chromosomal similarity is roughly equivalent to that found in equines (horses).

Interbreeding of horses and donkeys is common, although sterility of the offspring (*mules*) is nearly universal (with only around 60 exceptions recorded in equine history. Similar complexities and prevalent sterility pertain to horse-zebra hybrids, or *zorses*, whose chromosomal disparity is very wide, with horses typically having 32 chromosome pairs and zebras between 16 and 23 depending on species. [17]

Under an alternative and more technical classification, we define *intra-specific, inter-specific, inter-generic,* and *inter-ordinal hybrids.*

(5) Hybrids between different subspecies within a species (for example, Bengal tiger and Siberian tiger) are known as *intra-specific hybrids.* In other words, in this case we are dealing with *epigenic modification.* [18, 19]

HYBRID OF BENGAL TIGER AND SIBERIAN TIGER

Increasing interest in epigenetics has been accompanied by technological breakthroughs that now make it possible to undertake large-scale *epigenomic* studies. These allow the mapping of epigenetic marks, such as *DNA methylation, histone modifications* and *nucleosome positioning*, which are critical for regulating gene and noncoding RNA expression. In turn, we are learning how aberrant placement of these epigenetic marks and mutations in the epigenetic machinery is involved in disease. A comprehensive understanding of epigenetic mechanisms, their interactions and alterations in health and disease, has become a priority in biomedical research.

(6) Hybrids between different species within the same genus (for example, lions and tigers) are known as *inter-specific* hybrids or *crosses*. In this case of hybridization, the selection of the parental gender and ploidy are strongly

Primula sieboldii   **Primula kisoana**   **Triploid Hybrid**

related. For example, in reciprocal crosses of *Primula sieboldii* and *Primula kisoana,* when *P. sieboldii* is used as the maternal parent, the inter-specific hybrids are triploids (page 20); whereas, when *P. kisoana* is the maternal parent, the inter-specific hybrids were diploids.[20] The possibility of diploid female gamete formation in *P. sieboldii* is discussed as a causal factor in the production of triploids occasionally found in crosses between diploids of this species.

Primula sieboldii   **Primula kisoana**   **Diploid Hybrid**

(7) Hybrids between different genera (between sheep and goats, for example) are known as *intergeneric hybrids.*

21

INTERGENERIC HYBRID

(8) Extremely rare *interfamilial hybrids* have been known to occur; such as the guinea-fowl hybrids. It is the crossing between populations, breeds or cultivars within a single species. No interordinal hybrids (between different orders) are known.

Another classification is based on the parental treats: dominant and recessive. Accordingly, we appreciate single, double, and triple-cross hybrids.

(9) *Single cross hybrids* result from the cross between two true breeding organisms to produce an F1 generation or F1-hybrid (as in Final-1 or first offspring).

Guinea-fowl, INTRAFAMILIAL HYBRID

The cross between two different *homozygous* lines produces an F1 hybrid that is *heterozygous*; having two alleles, one contributed by each parent and typically one is dominant and the other recessive.

The F1 generation is also phenotypically homogeneous, producing offspring that are all similar to each other. An example is the selection of hybrids from two-eared maize populations.

23

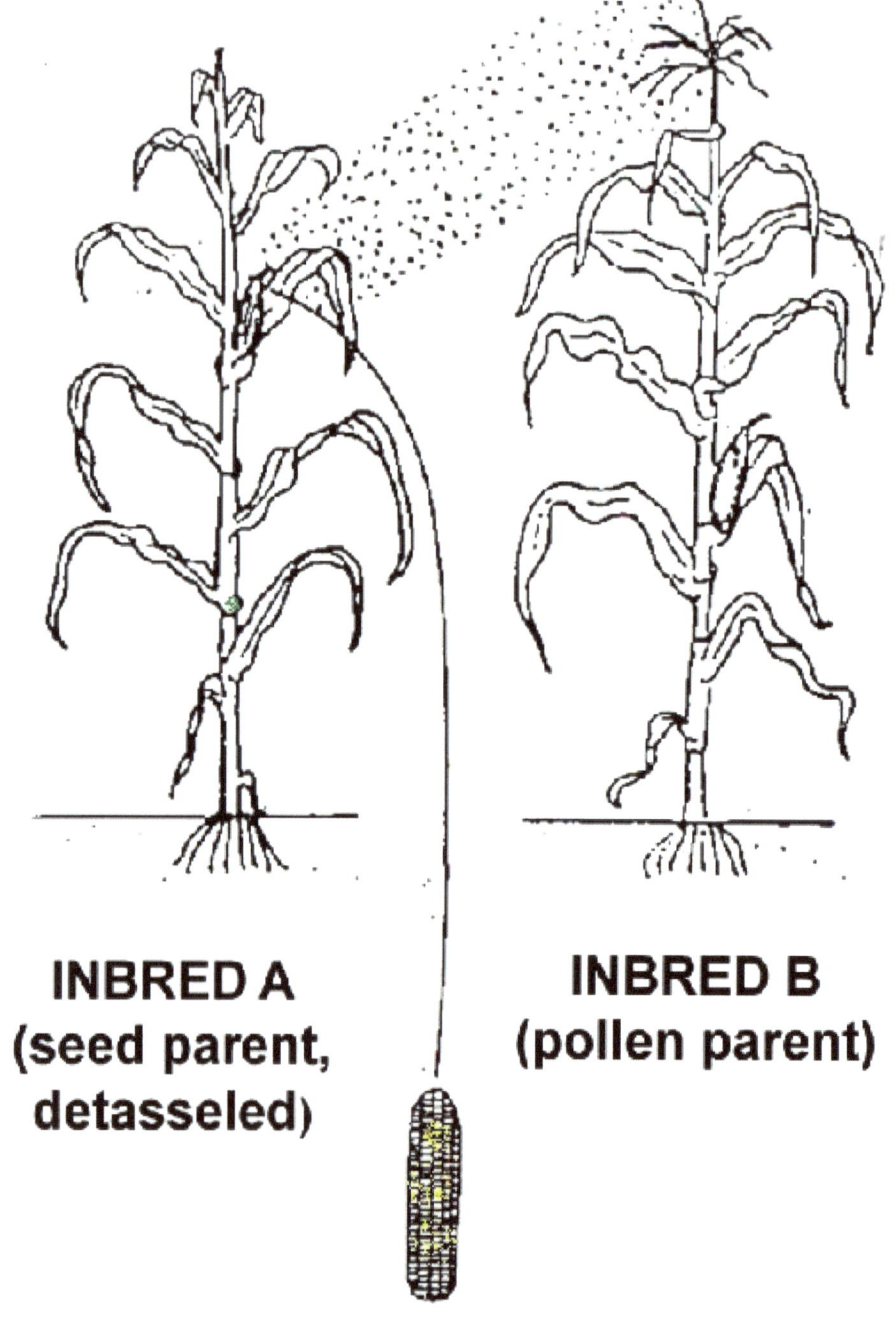

INBRED A
(seed parent,
detasseled)

INBRED B
(pollen parent)

SINGLE CROSS HYBRID SEED (A x B)

Selections are made among individual plant crosses in each generation of inbreeding. Selection among individual plant genotypes is continued until the plants are relatively homozygous, at which time one should have a group of selected single-cross hybrids that have been tested at each level of inbreeding.

SINGLE-CROSS HYBRID

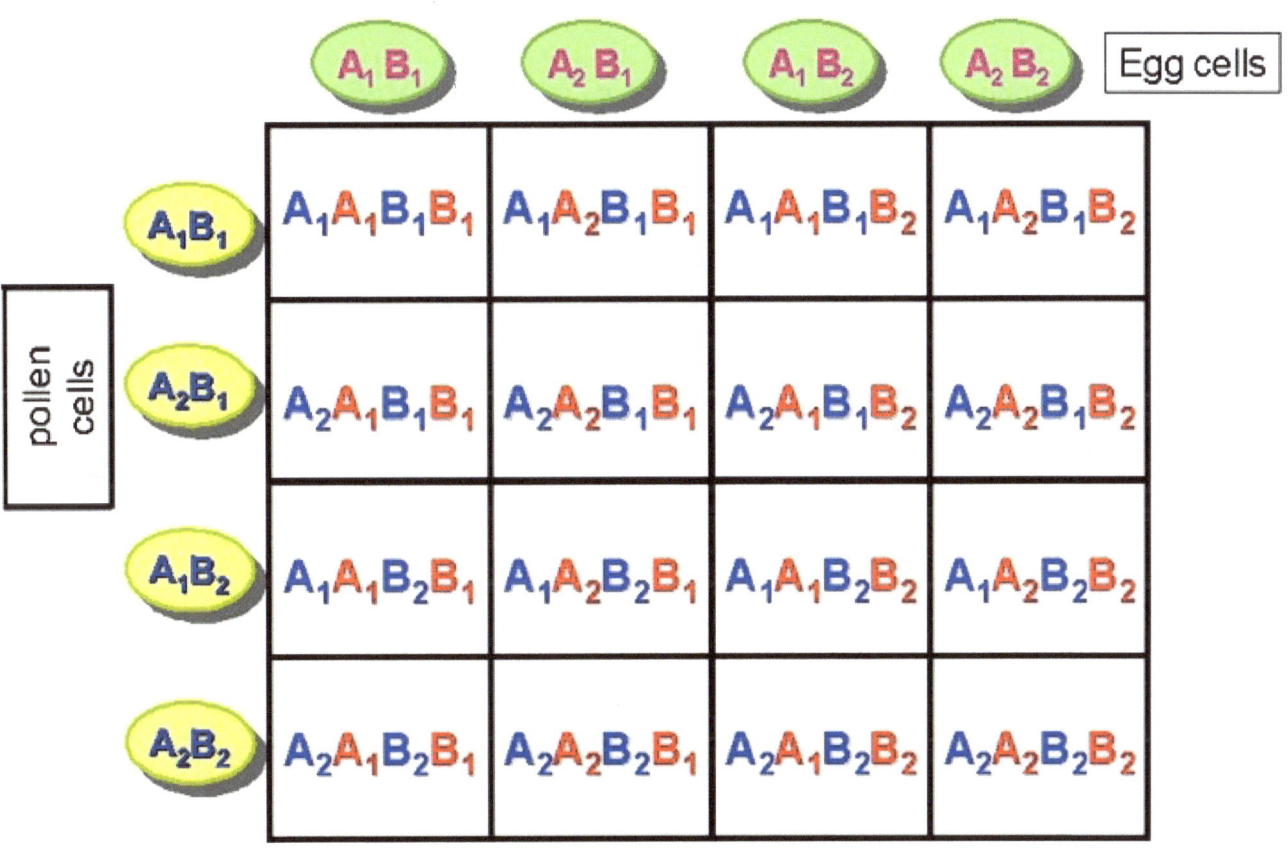

Two locus segregation

The procedure is designed to maximize selection for non-additive genetic effects.[21]

- *Double cross hybrids* result from the cross between two different F1 hybrids. The most prevalent type of hybrid that was grown in the United States in the 1930's was a double-cross hybrid.[22] Compared to single-cross hybrids, production of *double-cross* requires an extra step. It is a two-stage crossing involving two pairs of inbreds. In Step 1, two pairs of inbreds, A and B and Y and Z, are crossed to produce single-cross hybrids,

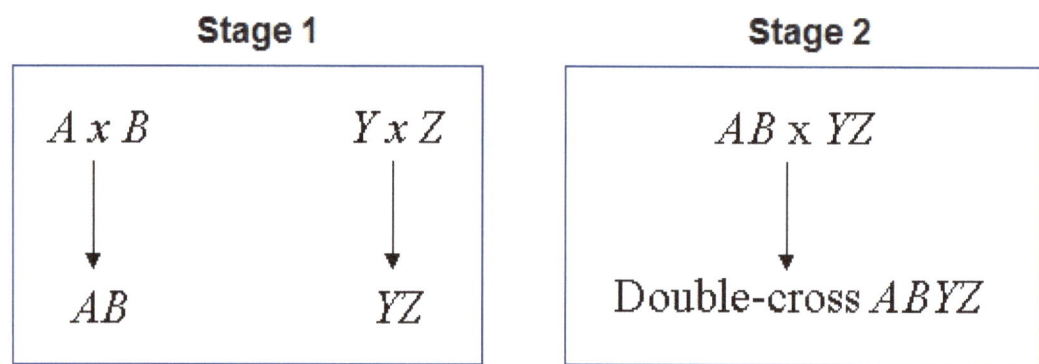

DOUBLE-CROSS HYBRID PRODUCTION

AB and YZ. In Step 2, the two single-cross hybrids produced in Step 1 are crossed to produce the double-cross. Typically, A and B are closely related and Y and Z are also closely related, but neither A nor B is closely related to Y or Z.

Unlike a single-cross hybrid, plants of a double-cross hybrid are not genetically uniform.

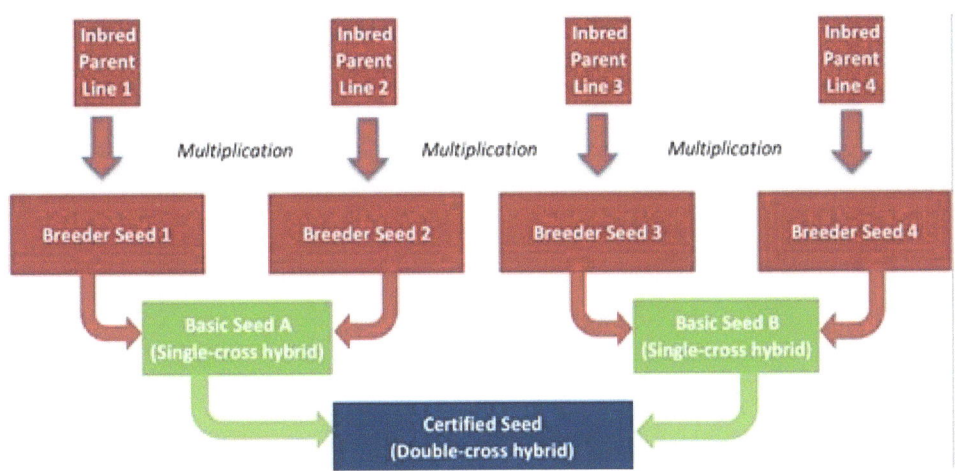

- *Three-way cross hybrids* result from the crossing between one parent that is an F1 hybrid and the other is from an inbred line. [23] The practical implication of this heterosis is very broad. Three-way and double cross hybrids can be used in pepper hybrid breeding. Selection of inbred lines for crossing from a similar market group can decrease heterogeneity in these categories of hybrids. [24] An example is crossing of *habanero* with *bell pepper:*

A x B   C x D
↓   ↓
AB   CD
\\   /
ABCD

Three-way crossing of *habanero* with *bell pepper*

- *Triple-cross hybrids* are produced from the crossing of two different three-way cross hybrids. On an example of the maize selection, this process consists of four stages: selection, popularization of open-pollinated varieties, intervarietal hybrid, and triple-cross hybrid. [25] *Pineberry* is another example of a triple hybrid of *Fragaria chiloensis* (costal strawberry) and *Fragaria virginiana* (Virginia wild strawberry):

(10) *Population hybrids* result from the crossing of plants or animals in a population with another population. These include inter-species and inter-racial crossings. Naturally occurring hybrid populations have characteristic traits that distinguish them from pure populations unaffected by hybridization. Certain of

these traits are important in *stabilization theory*. An example of on pisces population crossing is provided below:

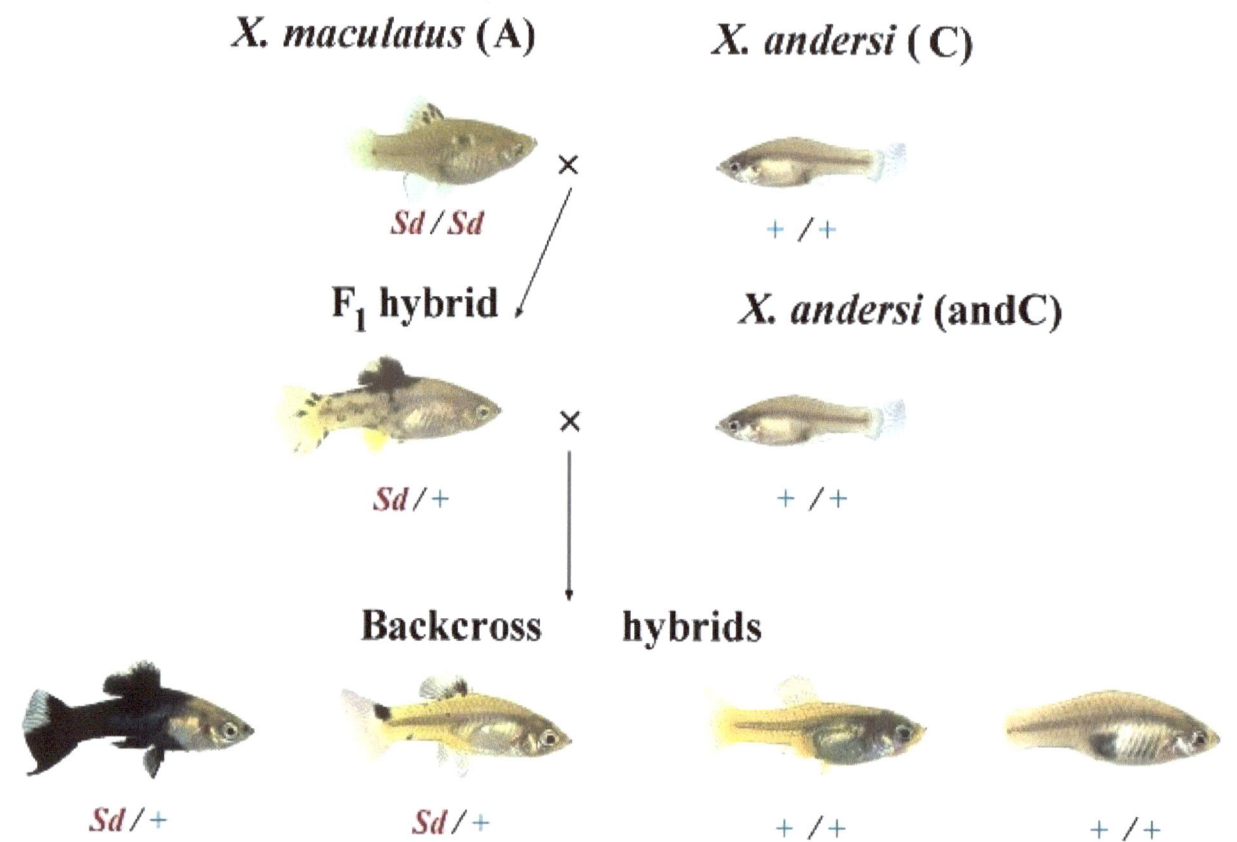

Our understanding of *population hybrids* is incomplete without defining the *hybrid zone, compound hybrid zone, mobile zone,* or *split ranges.*

The *hybrid zone* is a geographic region where genetically distinct natural populations come into contact, and hybridize. It is found in all major groups of the gametal organisms. The pure parental populations on opposite sides of a hybrid zone may differ with respect to almost any type of characteristic — appearance, behavior, physiology, or call.

Many hybrid populations exhibit a continuum of variation, spanning the gap between parental types. Within a population composed of partially fertile hybrids, the hybrids occupying regions closer to a particular parental type tend to be more similar to that parent. For example, a broad hybrid population between the Bush Squirrel (*Paraxerus cepapi*) and Red Bush Squirrel (*Paraxerus palliatus*) extends from southern Tanzania through Mozambique and Malawi to northeastern South Africa.

 +  =

Bush Squirrel
(*Paraxerus cepapi*)   **Red Bush Squirrel**
(*Paraxerus palliatus*)   **Hybrid**

Hybrid squirrels occurring near the range of Smith's Bush Squirrel have almost all the traits of *Paraxerus cepapi*. Those occurring near the Red Bush Squirrel have almost all those of *Paraxerus palliatus*. In intermediate regions there are squirrels of all intermediate types.

Similarly, in southwestern Guinea there is a hybrid zone between the Greater Bird of Paradise (*Paradisaea apoda*) and the Raggiana Bird of Paradise (*Paradisaea raggiana*). In this zone, birds vary geographically in appearance, from very similar to the Raggiana in the east to almost identical to the Greater in the west.

 +  =

Greater Bird of Paradise
(*Paradisaea apoda*)

Raggiana Bird of Paradise
(*Paradisaea raggiana*)

Double-wired hybrid

In Brazil, there is a hybrid zone between two primates, the Saddle-backed and White-mantled tamarins (*Saguinus fuscicollis* and *Saguinus melanoleucus*), in which again, hybrids of all degrees of intermediacy occur:

Saddle-backed tamarin
(Saguinus fuscicollis)
White-mantled tamarin
(Saguinus melanoleucus)
Hybrid

Compound Hybrid Zone: Compound hybrids, produced from crosses between multiple types of organisms, occur naturally in *compound hybrid zones* -- contact zones where multiple types interbreed. For example, three hummingbirds — the Purple-throated, White-throated, and Grey-tailed mountain-gems (*Lampornis calolaema, L. castaneoventris,* and *L. cinereicauda*) — have a three-way zone in southern Central America.

Purple-throated hummingbird
(Lampornis calolaema)

White-throated hummingbird
(Lampornis castaneoventris)

Grey-tailed hummingbird
(Lampornis cinereicauda)

In eastern Australia, five birds *sittellas* of the genus *Daphoenositta*, each distinct in appearance, hybridize where they come into contact along five lines radiating from a juncture in central Queensland. The birds in the hybrid population, near this center, may have ancestry involving all five different forms. In eastern Africa there are compound hybrid zones between distinct types of giraffes.

Mobile Zones: Most of the natural hybrid zones are mobile. The *hybrid zone* in eastern North America between the golden-winged and blue-winged warblers

(Vermivora chrysoptera and Vermivora pinus) moves every year, with V. pinus slowly taking over territory from the V. chrysoptera:

Golden-winged warbler
(Vermivora chrysoptera)

Blue-winged warbler
(Vermivora pinus)

Split Ranges: Since movement of a hybrid zone results from one of the hybridizing forms taking over range from the other, there is always the potential for the receding form's range to be split. The advancing zone might reach a coastline, mountain range, or river. Under such circumstances, the distribution of the receding form would become *discontinuous*, splitting on either side of the

Turquoise jay
(Cyanolyca turcosa)

Collared jay
(Cyanolyca viridicyana)

range of the advancing one. This process probably accounts for many situations where one organism has two ranges separated by the

range of another. Examples are such hybridizing pairs as the Turquoise and

Hooded crow
(Corvus cornix)

Carrion crow
(Corvus corone)

Collared jays (*Cyanolyca turcosa* and *Cyanolyca viridicyana*) of Peru, or the Hooded and Carrion crows (*Corvus cornix* and *Corvus corone*) of the Eurasian Ural. In the latter case, the one of crow hybridization, there are two hybrid zones some 4,000 kilometers apart, one in western Europe, the other in Asia. The range of the Hooded Crow lies in between.

Wide Zones and Hybrid Populations: When hybrids occur only at low frequency, parental populations can overlap broadly without significant genetic consequence. For example, the Mourning Warbler (*Oporornis philadelphia*) and

Mourning Warbler
(*Oporornis philadelphia*)

Canada Warbler
(*Wilsonia canadensis*)

Canada Warbler (*Wilsonia canadensis*) have almost identical breeding ranges in Canada and the northeastern United States. But, because there are only a few reports of hybridization between them, the situation appears stable. Levels of hybridization in this case do not appear to be high enough to significantly affect either population. On the other hand, if mixed matings produce progeny at higher rates, and those offspring are more fertile and viable, extensive hybrid populations can arise. [26]

There is a *wide zone* in southern Tanzania and northern Mozambique between the Checkered Elephant-Shrew (*Rhynchocyon cirnei*) and the Black-and-rufous Elephant-Shrew (*Rhynchocyon petersi*). This zone is so extended that pure

**Checkered Elephant-Shrew
(*Rhynchocyon cirnei*)**   **Black-and-rufous Elephant-Shrew
(*Rhynchocyon petersi*)**

parental individuals almost never come into contact to produce hybrids. In such cases virtually all individuals within the zone are later-generation hybrids.

Similar findings are reported regarding the hybrids between the European Hare (*Lepus europaeus*) and Mountain Hare (*Lepus timidus*) in Sweden. [27]

European Hare
(*Lepus europaeus*)

Mountain Hare
(*Lepus timidus*)

The width of a hybrid zone depends in part on the viability and fertility of the hybrids. The more infertile and inviable the species are, the narrower is the zone --if all other factors are equal. This makes sense, as if a hybrid zone is seen

Ramphastos toucans

as a population, it would be expected to grow if the hybrids were fitter. Even in crosses where the hybrids are quite fit, a hybrid zone may act to isolate the parental types from each other — the zone is so wide that they are isolated by distance. The extremely wide hybrid zones between *Ramphastos* toucans are an example.

HETEROSIS: Hybrids are often stronger than either parent variety, a phenomenon most common with plant hybrids, known as *hybrid vigor* (heterosis) or *heterozygote advantage* (see page 13). A transgressive phenotype is a phenotype displaying more extreme characteristics than either of the parent lines. An economically important example is hybrid maize (corn), which provides a considerable seed yield advantage over open pollinated varieties. Hybrid seed dominates the commercial maize seed market in the United States, Canada and many other major maize producing countries. [28, 29]

INTERGRADATION: Natural hybridization or heterosis is often referred to as *intergradation,* especially in cases where there is *clinal variation.* A *cline* is a graded series of differences exhibited within a population -- usually along a geographic line or across a region of environmental transition. In the east coast

White-tailed deer
(*Odocoileus virginianus*)

of North America, white-tailed deer (*Odocoileus virginianus*) gradually declines in size from north to south.

Intergradation came to be applied to hybridization between populations since the variation in such cases is commonly *clinal* in nature. Hybrid populations often have a very broad geographic distribution. The rate of change across such a population may be very gradual. Thus, four South American toucans often treated as species (Ramphastos ariel, R. citreolaemus, R. culminatus, and R. vitellinus) are

Ramphastos ariel **Ramphastos citreolaemus**

Ramphastos culminatus **Ramphastos vitellinus**

recognizable as types within their respective ranges, but are separated by huge hybrid populations more than a thousand kilometers wide.

Under such circumstances use of the term intergradation makes sense because the populations merge gradually, one with the other, through a continuous series of intermediate individuals. However, the word is also often applied in the case of populations that interbreed regularly but maintain a sharp discontinuous boundary where they interface.

While the Hoffmann's Woodpecker (*Melanerpes hoffmannii*) and the Red-crowned Woodpecker (*Melanerpes rubricapillus*) each have extensive ranges, they

Hoffmann's Woodpecker
(*Melanerpes hoffmannii*)

Red-crowned Woodpecker
(*Melanerpes rubricapillus*)

often *inter-grade* in Costa Rica because they hybridize in that peculiar region. We have to appreciate, that in this case ther's inter-breeding without gradual transition.

The traits of these birds have remained sharply distinct and their *hybrid zone* is quite narrow. Using *intergrade* instead of *hybridize* is misleading in description of sharply distinct populations, because such populations are erroneously supposed to blend via a wide hybrid population, when they don't.

Note: in this monograph, the word *hybridization* refers to interbreeding of all kinds, regardless the broad *cline* production between the affected populations.

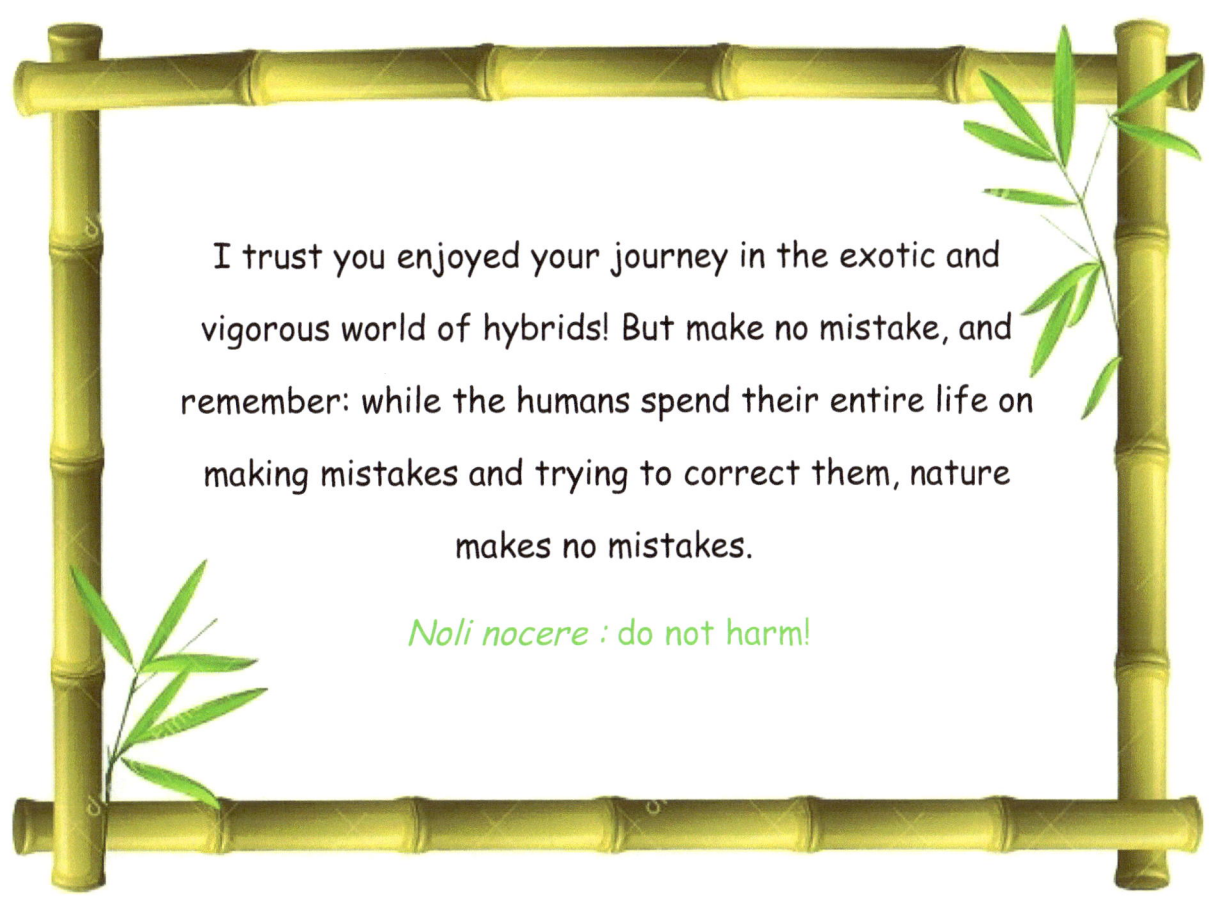

I trust you enjoyed your journey in the exotic and vigorous world of hybrids! But make no mistake, and remember: while the humans spend their entire life on making mistakes and trying to correct them, nature makes no mistakes.

Noli nocere : do not harm!

REFERENCES:

(1) Oxford English Dictionary Online, Oxford University Press , 2007

(2) Culumber ZW, Ochoa OM, Rosenthal GG (2014). .Assortative mating and the maintenance of population structure in a natural hybrid zone. *The American Naturalist*;184(2):225-32.

(3) Susumu O, Junich M, Lawrence C, Niels AB. (1967). Diploid–tetraploid relationship among old-world members of the fish family *Cyprinidae*. *Chromosoma*; 23 (1): 1–9

(4) Bertolani R (2001). Evolution of the reproductive mechanisms in Tardigrades: a review. *Zoologischer Anzeiger;* 240 (3–4): 247–252

(5) Mable BK, Alexandrou MA, Taylor MI. (2011). Genome duplication in amphibians and fish: an extended synthesis. *Journal of Zoology*; 284: 151–182.

(6) Nobel Prize in Physiology or Medicine 2012 Awarded for Discovery That Mature Cells Can Be Reprogrammed to Become Pluripotent". *ScienceDaily;* October 08, 2012.

(7) Winkelmann M, Pfitzer P, Schneider W (1987). Significance of polyploidy in megakaryocytes and other cells in health and tumor disease. *Klinische Wochenschrift;* 65 (23): 1115–31

(8) McDaniel SF, Willis JH, Shaw J (2008). The genetic basis of developmental abnormalities in interpopulation hybrids of the moss Ceratodon purpureus. *Genetics;* 179(3): 1425–1435.

(9) Vause KE, McDougall JK (1973). Identification of group `E' chromosome abnormalities in human cells . *Journal of Medical Genetics;* 10(1): 70–73

(10) Hurt K, Sottner O, Záhumenský J, et al. (2007). Choroid plexus cysts and risk of trisomy 18. Modifications regarding maternal age and markers. *Ceska Gynekologica;* 72 (1): 49–52

(11) Papp C, Ban Z, Szigeti Z,et al (2007). Role of second trimester sonography in detecting trisomy 18: a review of 70 cases. *Journal of Clinical Ultrasound;* 35 (2): 68–72

(12) Rodeck CH, Whittle MJ (1999). Fetal medicine: Basic science and clinical practice. *Elsevier Health Sciences* (Paperback)

(13) Halbert, ND, Ward TJ, Schnabel RD, et al (2005). Conservation genomics: disequilibrium mapping of domestic cattle chromosomal segments in North American bison populations. *Molecular Ecology;* 14, 2343–2362

(14) Jdo JW, Baldini A, Ward DC, et al (1991). Origin of human chromosome 2: an ancestral telomere-telomere fusion. *Proc. National. Academy Science;* 88 (20): 9051– 5

(15) Resnik DB (2003). Patents on human-animal chimeras and threats to human dignity. The *American Journal of Bioethics;* 3(3)

(16) Rossiianov, K (2002). Beyond species: Il'ya Ivanov and his experiments on cross-breeding humans with anthropoid apes. *Science in Context;* 15 (2): 277–316

(17) Wimmer R, Kirsch S, Rappold GA, Schempp W (2002). Direct evidence for a Pan-Homo clade. *Chromosome Research;* 10 (1): 55–61

(18) Xinxin Z, Yang Ch, Bao L (2007). Epigenetic inheritance and variation of DNA methylation level and pattern in maize intra-specific hybrids. *Plant Science;* 172 (5): 930-938

(19) Portela A, Esteller M (2010). Epigenetic modifications and human disease. Nature *Biotechnology;* 28: 1057-1068

(20) Mii M, Kato J (2000). Differences in ploidy levels of inter-specific hybrids obtained by reciprocal crosses between Primula sieboldii and P. kisoana. *Theoretical and Applied Genetics;* 101(5-6): 690-696

(21) Hallauer AR (1967). Development of single-cross hybrids from two-eared maize populations. *American Society of Agronomy;* 7(3):192-195

(22) USDA/NIFA (2014). Corn breeding: Types of cultivars. *Plant and Soil Sciences e-Libary[Pro]*

(23) Rawlings JO, Cockerham C (1962). Analysis of double cross hybrid populations. *Biometrics*, 18(2): 229–244

(24) Geleta LF, Labuschagne MT (2004). Comparative performance and heterosis in single, three-way and double cross pepper hybrids. *The Journal of Agricultural Science*, 142(6):659–663

(25) Li SK, Wang CT (2009). Evolution and development of maize production techniques in China. *Scientia Agricultura Sinica;* 42(6):1941–1951

(26) Shotake T (1981). Population genetic study of natural hybridization between *Papio anubis* and *P. hamadryas. Primates;* 22(3):285–308

(27) Thulin CG, Fang M, Averianov A (2006). Introgression from Lepus europaeus to L. timidus in Russia revealed by mitochondrial single nucleotide polymorphisms and nuclear microsatellites. *Hereditas* ; 143 (2006): 68–76.

(28) Stokes D, Morgan C, O'Neill C, Bancroft I (2007). Evaluating the utility of Arabidopsis thaliana as a model for understanding heterosis in hybrid crops. *Euphytica;* 156(1–2):157–171

(29) Wayne SC (2004) *Corn: Origin, history, technology, and production. Wiley Series in Crop Science;* 332.

www.ingramcontent.com/pod-product-compliance
Lightning Source LLC
Chambersburg PA
CBHW041516280526
45792CB00004B/1273